SMART BRAIN RIGHT BRAIN

Let's Measure

First Published in 2021 by

Om Books International

Corporate & Editorial Office
A-12, Sector 64, Noida 201 301
Uttar Pradesh, India
Phone: +91 120 477 4100
Email: editorial@ombooks.com
Website: www.ombooksinternational.com

Sales Office
107, Ansari Road, Darya Ganj
New Delhi 110 002, India
Phone: +91 11 4000 9000
Email: sales@ombooks.com

Author: Shweta Sinha
Editor: Kirti Pathak
Art & Design: Anshuman Pandey, Gaurav Bhandari, Harish Arya

ISBN: 978-93-5276-858-5

Printed in India

10 9 8 7 6 5 4 3 2 1

CONTENTS

1. Measuring Things

Here are some ways we describe things around us:

Tall, short, big, small, long, heavy are all words to describe sizes. However, these words do not tell us exactly how big or small something is.

POCKET FACT

We use measurements everyday at home, school and in office.

In order to have precise measurements you need to compare sizes to a fixed standard. A standard is an amount that remains the same all the time. When you use standards, everyone knows exactly how much you mean. A standard uses numbers and units to show the size or amount of something.

Units Of Measurement

We follow two basic measurement systems.

The **metric system** was designed to be easy to work with since it uses 10s, 100s and 1000s. Most countries follow the metric system nowadays. Metre, kilogram and litre are some of the commonly used units of measurement.	The **imperial system** was the traditional system and it uses different amounts to divide different units. This system is still followed in the US and some parts of UK. Inch, feet, pound, ounce and gallon are some of the commonly used units of measurements.

DID YOU KNOW? A kilometre is the same length, and a kilogram is the same weight everywhere in the world.

2. How Long?

Length is a measure that answers these questions.

How tall is my plant?

How long is this shoe?

How wide are my arms?

How thick are these books?

POCKET FACT

Height is the distance between the lowest and highest points of a person or an object.

How far is grandma's house?

How high is the mountain?

How deep is the ocean?

DID YOU KNOW?

In ancient times, people took measurements using the length of their foot, width of a finger or the distance of a step.

Units of Length

When we measure length, we need to choose the best unit to work with.
An **inch**(in.) is a good choice when measuring small items such as books, pencils or coins. When measuring a computer screen or other medium length objects you can use **feet** (ft.) too.

Things that are about an inch long:

In the metric system, small and medium lengths are measured in millimetres (mm), centimetres (cm) and metres (m).

DID YOU KNOW?

A ruler is usually a foot long. Twelve inches make one foot.

For long distances we use **miles** (mi) or **kilometres** (km).

Maps are a smaller version of the real thing. They show big distances by scaling them down.

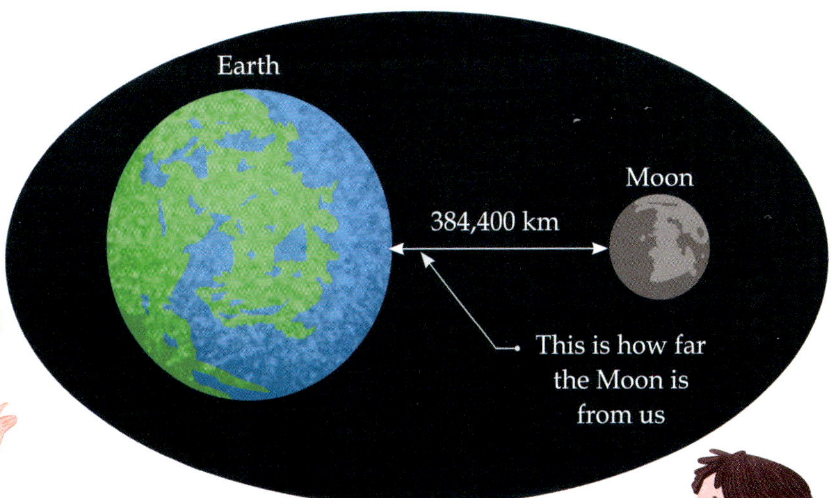

POCKET FACT

A millimetre is about the thickness of a credit card while a kilometre is the least distance most major roads cover.

3. Activity: How to Use a Ruler

To measure the length of things, you must know how to use and read a ruler. A ruler typically has inches marked on one side and centimetres on the other. Here you will learn to measure in metric units.

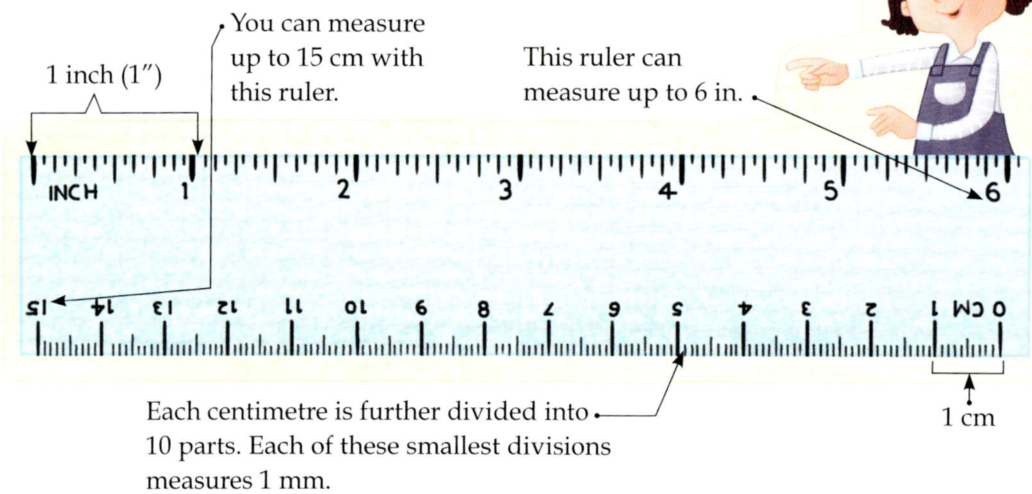

The distance between two consecutive numbers on the inch side measures 1 inch. Similarly, the distance between two consecutive numbers on the centimetres side measures exactly 1 cm.

Let's measure an unsharpened pencil.

Step 1. Place the 0 cm mark at one end of the unsharpened pencil. Do not measure from the end of the ruler.

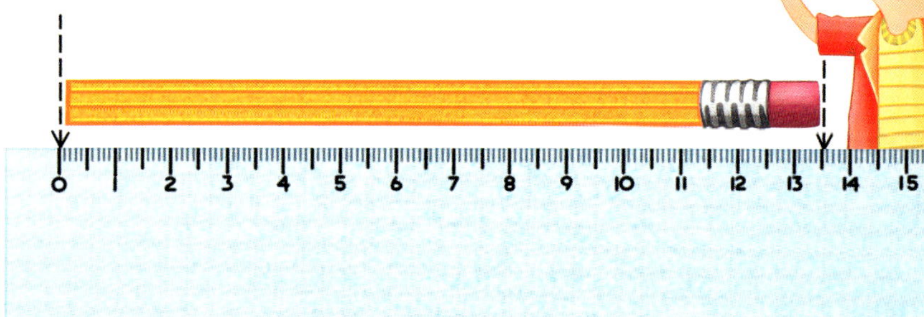

Step 2. To find the length, round the length down to the nearest number on the ruler.

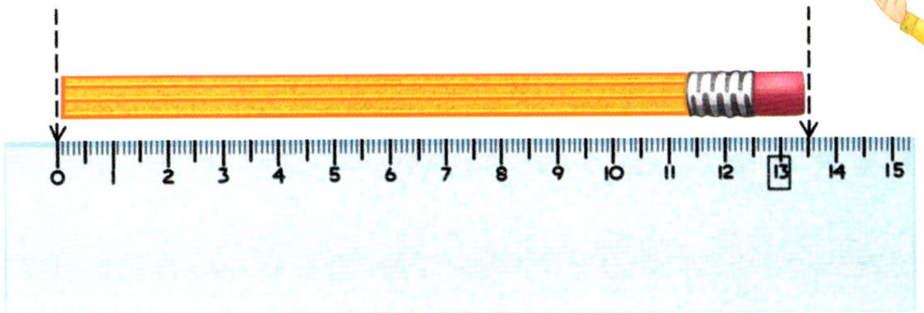

Step 3. Count the number of intervals after the whole number. This gives the millimetre reading.

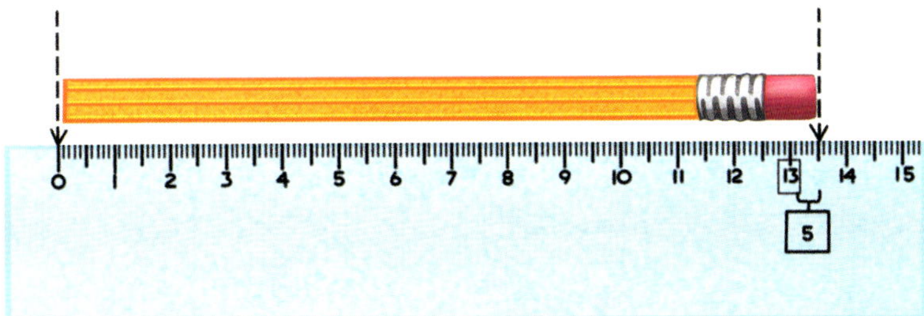

So, if the nearest number on the ruler is '13' and the small intervals after 13 till the end of the pencil is 5, the length of the pencil is 13 cm 5 mm.

Quiz

What is the length of this pencil?

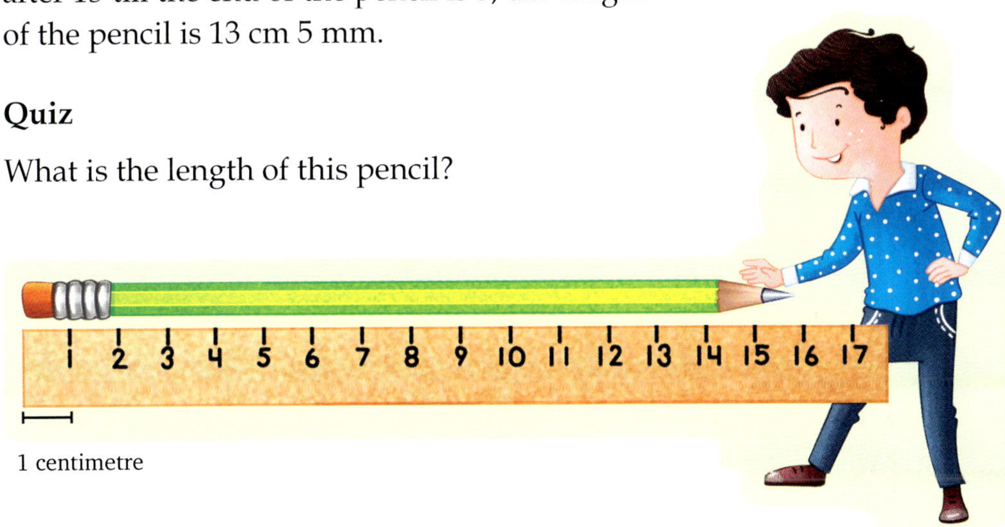

Answer: 16 cm

4. Measuring Mass

Mass is a measure of how much stuff an object has. Measuring weight means measuring the heaviness of an object. Weight actually tells how strongly the force of gravity pulls on the object. Gravity is what pulls us down on Earth.

How much does it **weigh**?

DID YOU KNOW?

Your weight on Moon, will be lesser than your weight on Earth. This is because the Moon has lesser gravitational pull than Earth.

Weight is measured in grams and kilograms. When using the imperial system, weight is measured in pounds and ounces.

A gram is very light. These things weigh about a gram each.

1 kilogram is a 1000 grams. These things weigh about a kilogram each.

Quiz

How many paper clips will weigh the same as a 1 litre bottle of water?

Answer:

Weight of 1 paper clip = 1 g

Weight of the bottle = 1 kg or 1000g

So, 1000 paper clips will weigh the same as the bottle of water.

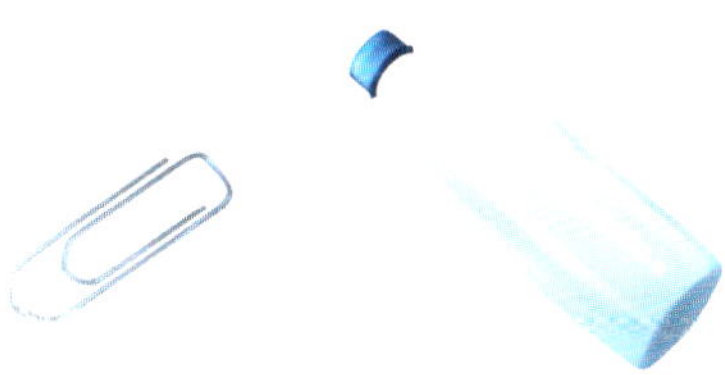

Types of Weighing Scales

You need **weighing scales** to measure the weight of any object. Weighing scales come in various types, sizes and shapes.

A **balance scale** is used to weigh objects by balancing them with standard weights. You can also use it to find out which is heavier among two objects.

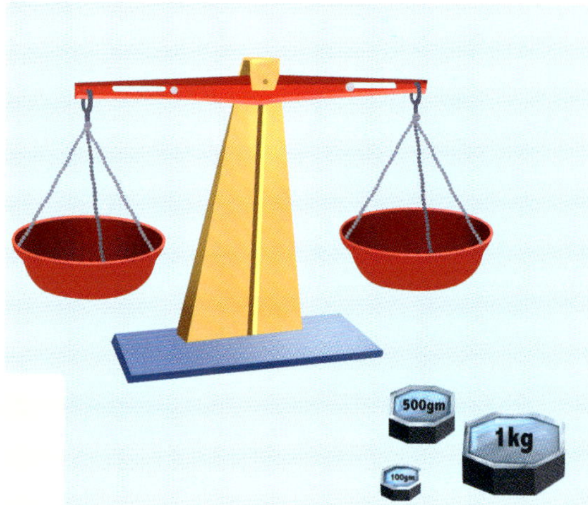

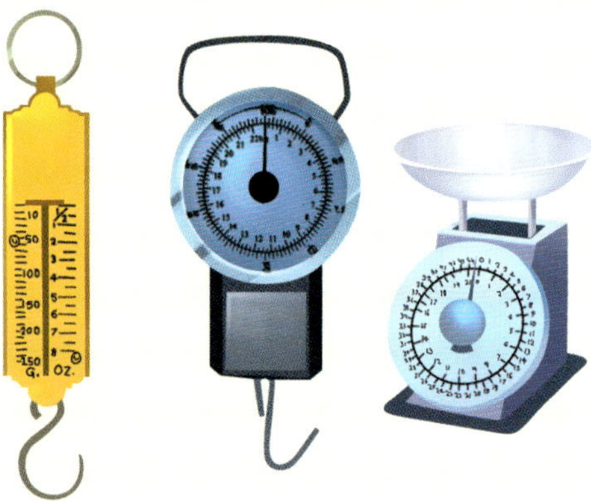

A **spring balance** uses a spring to measure weights of small objects.

A **platform scale** is used to measure weights of bigger objects. They often have a digital display. You may have weighed yourself on one such scale or seen one at an airport, weighing luggage.

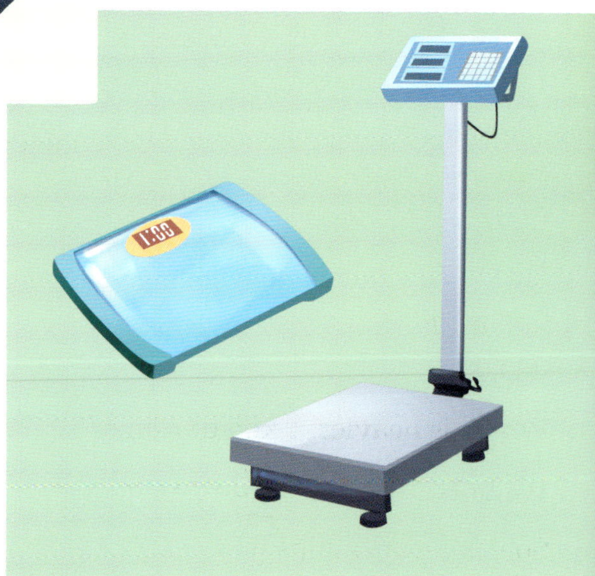

A **weigh bridge** is used to measure weights of trucks and other such large objects. Weigh bridges give weight in tons.

1 metric ton = 1000 kilograms (kg)

Quiz

Which is heavier: 1 kilo of iron or 1 kilo of feathers?

Answer: They weigh the same.

5. Capacity and Volume

The **capacity** of a container is the amount of stuff it can hold when full.

This box has a capacity of **5 books.**

This jug holds **6 glasses** of water when full.

10 shovels of sand fill up this bucket.

You cannot compare the capacity of these three objects shown on this page, as their units of measurements are not the same.

DID YOU KNOW?

Only hollow objects have capacity.

Volume is the amount of space something occupies. To find the volume of a liquid, you can pour it into a container and measure the space it occupies.

Amy and her friends came back from playing outside. They were thirsty, so they poured themselves some orange juice from a box.

Amy was mighty thirsty. She filled her **whole** glass with juice.

Peter wasn't fond of orange juice. He filled his glass **less than half-full**.

Camilla was left with only **half** a glass of juice.

Can you compare and find out who drank the most juice?

Yes you can, as all three glasses are of equal size, i.e., their units of measurements are the same.

However, to measure liquids accurately, we use a measuring cylinder. The units to measure volume are **millilitres (mL), litres (L) and fluid ounces (fl. oz)**.

The volume of liquid in this measuring cylinder is 125 mL.

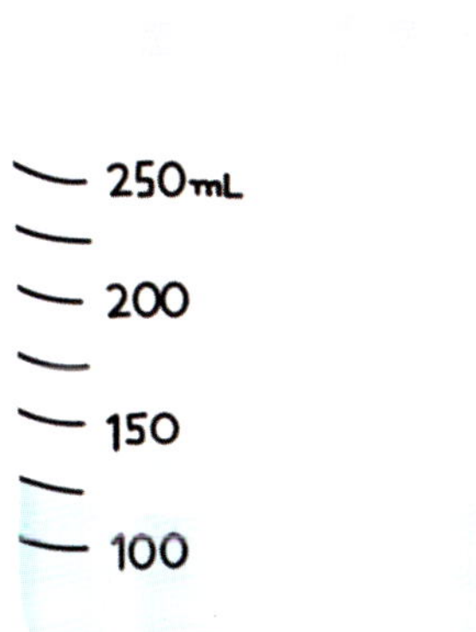

POCKET FACT

Litre is a metric unit while fluid ounce is an imperial unit. Gallons are used to measure a large quantity of liquid.

Volume of Solids

Solids have a fixed shape and they occupy a fixed space or volume. You can think of the volume of a solid shape as the amount of water it can hold when full. Both solid and hollow objects have volume. The volume of solids is measured in **cubic units** such as **cubic millimetres, cubic centimetres** and **cubic meters**.

A **millimetre cube** is about the size of a sugar cube. This unit measures very small volumes. It is also written as cu. mm or mm3.

A **centimetre cube** is used to measure bigger objects. One centimetre cube (cm3), also written as cu. cm, is about the size of a dice.

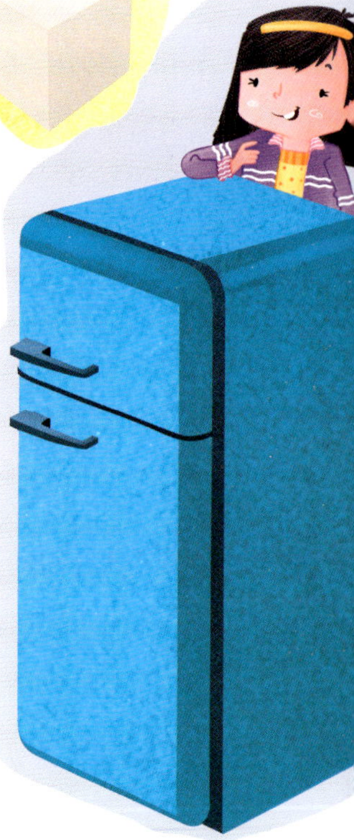

Refrigerators and other very large objects are measured in **metre cubes**. Metre cube is also written as m3 or cu. m.

DID YOU KNOW?

One gallon of milk weighs approximately 4 kilograms; while one litre of milk is about 1 kilogram.

Cubic inch (cu. in.) and cubic feet (cu. ft.) are the corresponding units for volume in the imperial system.

6. Activity: Volume of Irregular Solids

One way to measure the volume of a solid object is to submerge it in water and then measure the volume of water displaced by the object.

You need:

- A measuring cylinder or a beaker
- Water
- Stone to be measured. The stone should be small enough to fit in the measuring cylinder.

Step 1. Fill the measuring cylinder with sufficient water. Take a reading for the volume of water you poured by noting down the number value at the top surface of water.

Step 2. Drop the stone into the water.

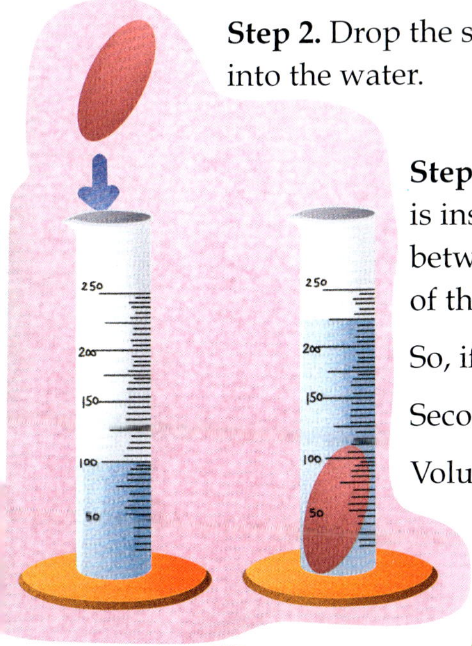

Step 3. Take the reading after the stone is inside the water. The difference between the two readings is the volume of the stone.

So, if the first reading = 100 mL

Second reading = 225 mL

Volume of the stone = 225 - 100 = 125 mL

7. Area and Perimeter

Area is the amount of space inside a flat shape. Small areas are calculated in units of square centimetres. Square kilometres are used to measure large areas such as the area of a city or a country.

A square centimetre is written as cm2 or sq. cm and a square metre is written as m2 or sq. m.

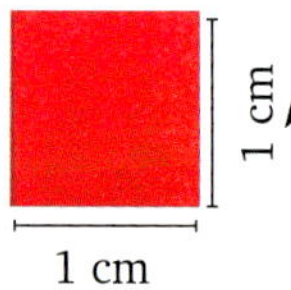

A sq. cm is a square with sides measuring 1 cm.

How many square centimetres can fit in this rectangle shape?

There are 15 squares in this shape. Hence, its area is equal to 15 sq. cm.

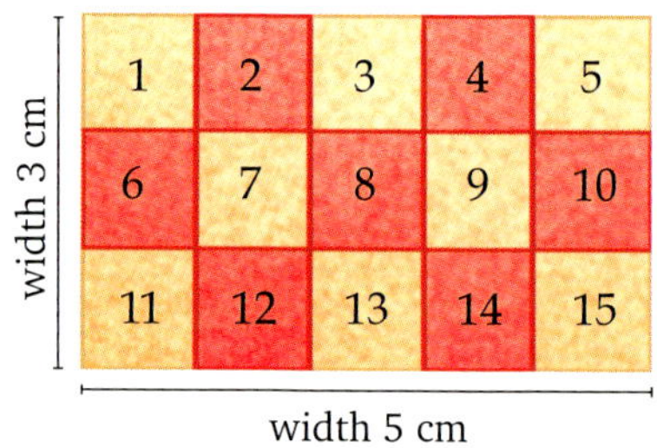

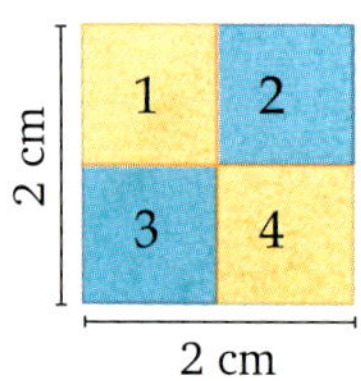

This square contains 4 squares. So, its area is 4 square centimeters.

Sometimes squares don't exactly match up to shapes. One way to find the area is to get an approximate answer.

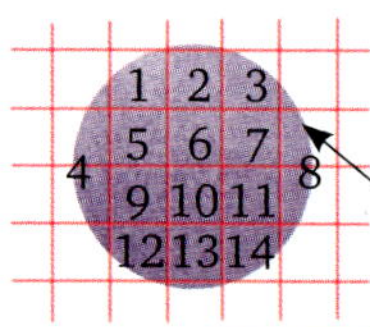

This circle is about 14 sq. cm.

POCKET FACT

The floor area of a room or a house is measured either in square metres or square feet.

A better method is to use formulae to calculate the area of 2-D shapes.

Shape	Name	Formula for Area
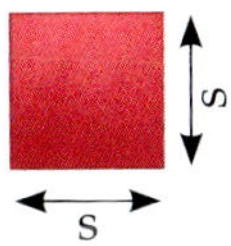	Square	Side = s **Area = s × s, or s^2**
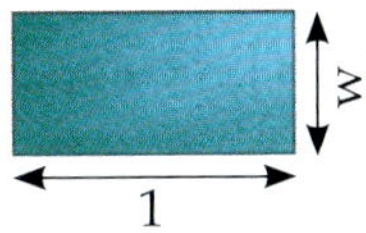	Rectangle	Length = l Width = w **Area = l × w**
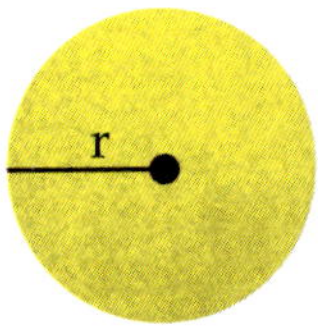	Circle	Radius = r (distance from the centre point to the edge of the circle) π (Pi) = 3.14, a constant number **Area=πr^2 or 3.14 × r × r**
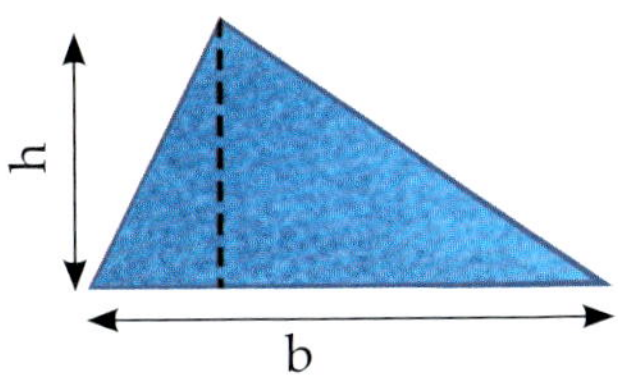	Triangle	Base = b Height = h **Area = (b × h) ÷2**

Quiz

What is the area of a square of side 10cm and a circle with a radius of 2cm?

Answer: Area of the square = 10cm × 10cm = $100cm^2$

Area of the circle = 3.14 × 2 cm × 2cm = 12.56 cm^2

Perimeter

Perimeter is the outline that surrounds a plane shape. It is the rim or the boundary of the shape.

Here is a simple activity to measure the perimeter of a square:

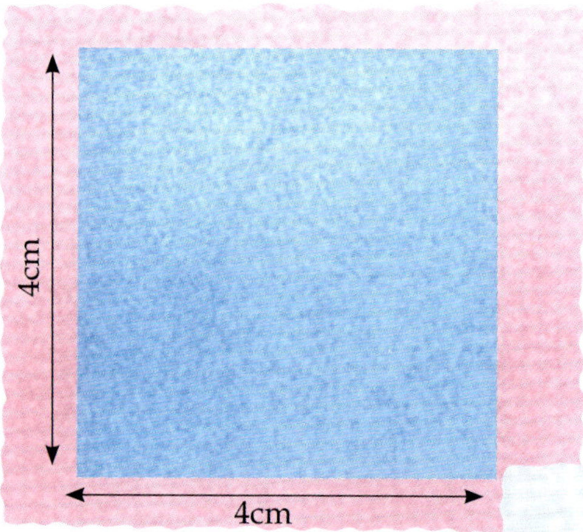

Step 1. Draw a square with sides 4 cm on a sheet of paper.

Step 2. Start by taking a string and placing one end on a corner of the square. Start placing the string along the path of the square. Take care not to move the end of the string from the corner.

Step 3. Continue around the square and stop when you reach the corner where you started.

Step 4. Mark the length of the string used to cover the square. Cut the string at this mark. You now have the string as long at the path of the square.

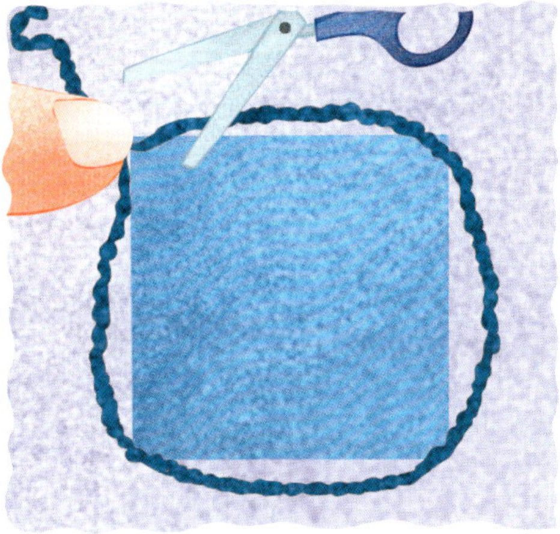

Step 5. Measure the length of the string using a ruler. This length is the perimeter. Your answer should be 16 cm.

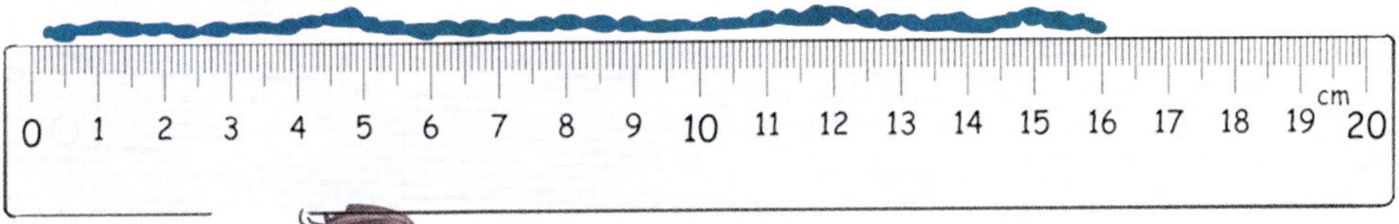

DID YOU KNOW?

The word perimeter comes from the Greek word peri, meaning around, and metron, meaning measure.

The perimeter is the total length of all sides of a two-dimensional shape. For regular shapes, like a square, you can measure the sides with a ruler and add up the values. For irregular shapes, use a string as described before to calculate the perimeter.

Perimeter is measured in cm, m, km, yards, feet, inches, etc. Like area, there are formulae to calculate the perimeter too.

Shape	Name	Formulae for Perimeter
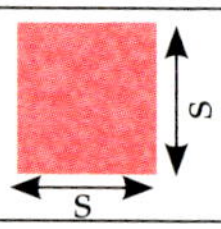	Square	Side = s **Perimeter = 4s**
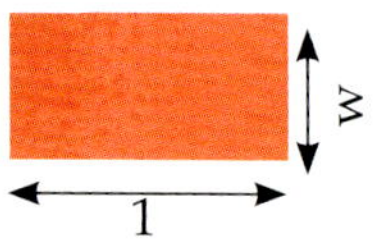	Rectangle	Length = l Width = w **Perimeter = 2(l + w)**
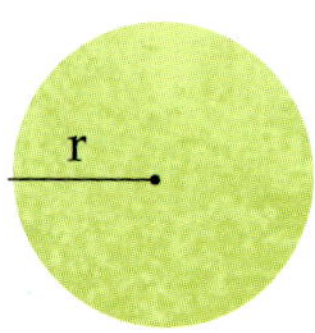	Circle	Radius = r (distance from the centre point to the edge of the circle) π (Pi) = 3.14, a constant number **Perimeter = 2 πr or 3.14 × 2r**
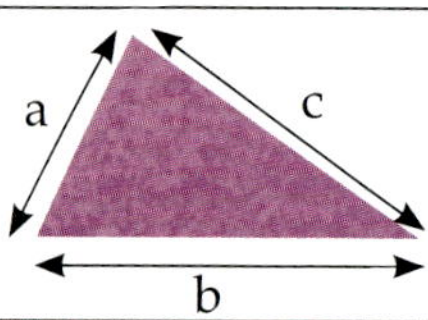	Triangle	Sides = a, b, c **Perimeter = a+b+c**

POCKET FACT

The perimeter of a circle is also called its circumference.

Area vs. Perimeter

Area and perimeter are both vital measures that define any flat shape. Both concepts have several practical applications in our lives. While area tells us how much space we have in our garden, we need to know its perimeter to fence the boundary.

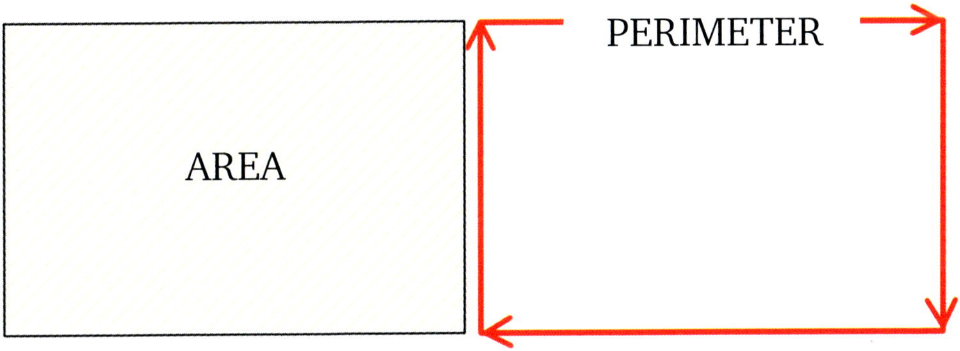

Key differences between area and perimeter:

- Area describes the amount of surface covered by an object, while perimeter is a measure of the outer edge.
- Area is measured in square units (sq. m, sq. km, sq. feet). Perimeter is measured in linear units (m, km, feet).
- Area involves two dimensions - length and width. While perimeter involves only one dimension, i.e., the total length.

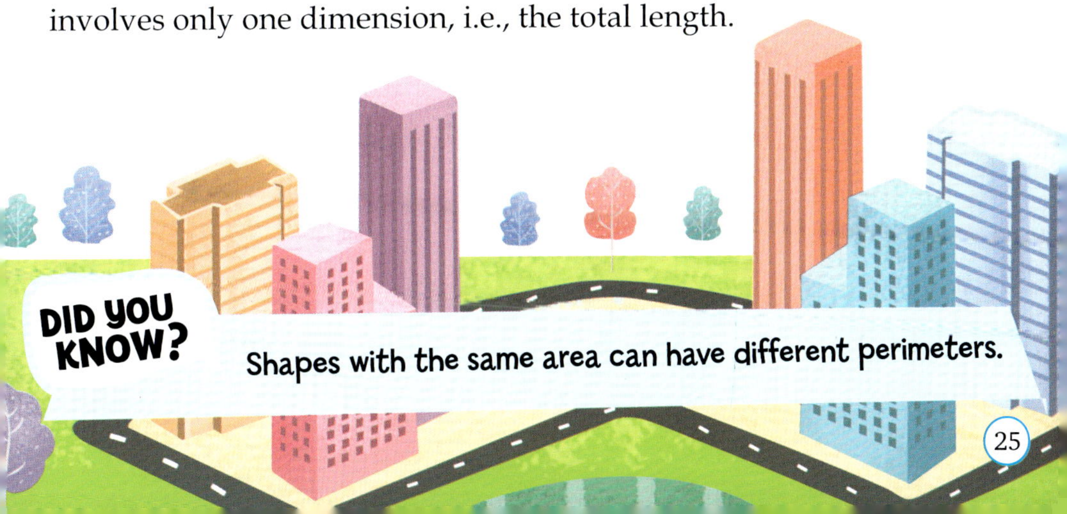

DID YOU KNOW? Shapes with the same area can have different perimeters.

8. Metric Unit Conversions

Metric units can be converted from one unit to another by multiplying or dividing by 10s, 100s or 1000s.

Units for Length

- 10 millimetres (mm) = 1 centimetre (cm) (about the diameter of an AAA battery)

- 100 centimetres (cm) = 1 metre (m) (about the length of a guitar)

- 1000 metres (m) = 1 kilometre (km) (about the distance of seven city blocks)

Other units for measuring length are:

- 1 decimetre (dm) = 10 centimetres (cm)
- 1 metre (m) = 10 decimetres (dm)
- 1 decametre (dam) = 10 metres (m)
- 1 hectometre (hm) = 10 decametre (dam)
- 1 kilometre (km) = 10 hectometre (hm)

DID YOU KNOW?

One micrometre (micron) is 1000 times smaller than a millimetre and cannot be measured with the naked eye. Dust particles are measured in microns.

Units for Weight

Units used to measure weight are milligram, centigram, decigram, gram, decagram, hectogram, kilogram.

- 1000 milligrams (mg) = 1 gram (g)
  (about the weight of a paper clip)

- 1000 grams (g) = 1 kilogram (kg)
  (about the weight of a bag of pasta)

1,000 paper clips

=

1 kg Pasta

Units for Capacity

Units used to measure capacity are millilitre, centilitre, decilitre, litre, dekalitre, hectolitre, kilolitre.

- 1000 millilitres (mL) = 1 litre (L)
  (about the volume of a 1L bottle of water)

Here is an easy way to remember the acronyms (kilo, centi, milli, etc.):

Multiply→

King	**H**ector	**D**oesn't	**U**sually	**D**rink	**C**hocolate	**M**ilk
kilo	**h**ecto	**d**eca	**u**nit	**d**eci	**c**enti	**m**illi

10 10 10 10 10 10

←Divide

POCKET FACT

A millilitre is about 20 drops of water.

× 20

Find the Length

Find the length of each bar. The ruler measures in cm and mm.

1.	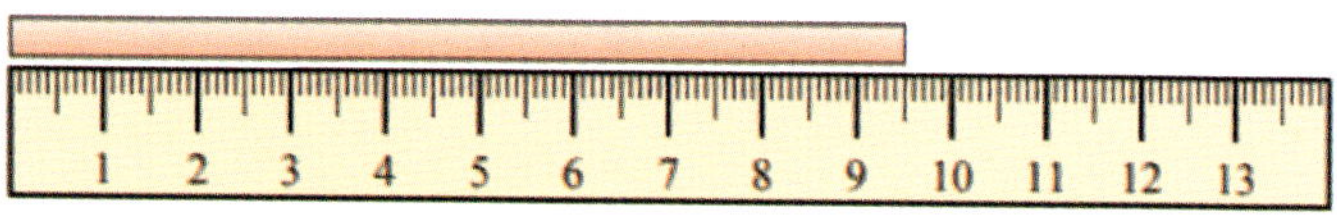	
2.		
3.	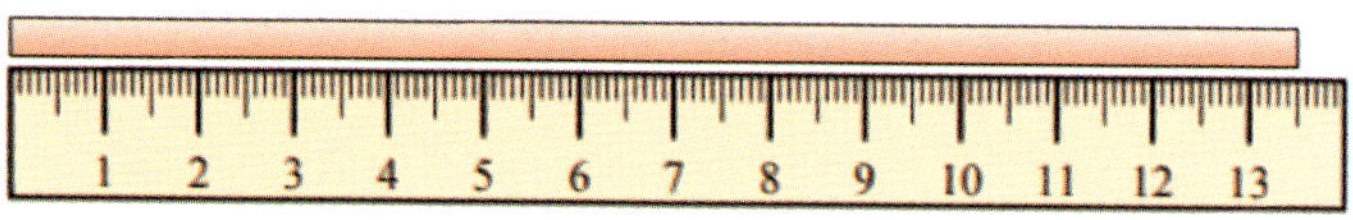	
4.	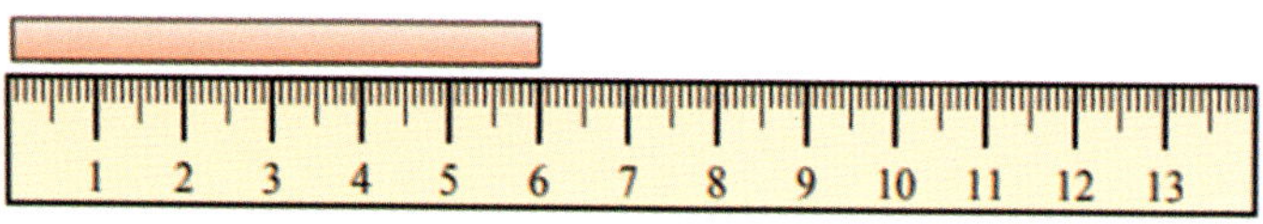	
5.		

Guess the Measurement

Choose the metric unit that best answers the question:

1. The approximate height of an apple is 10 metres or 10 centimetres?

2. The volume of soda in a can is 350 millilitres or 350 litres?

3. A kitten weighs around 1000 grams or 1000 kilograms?

4. The amount of water used to water a plant is 150 millilitres or 150 litres?

5. A gallon of milk weighs about 4 grams or 4 kilograms?

6. The depth of a swimming pool is 3 kilometres or 3 metres?

Metric Unit Conversion

1. 20 kilograms = ___________ grams

2. 60,000 metres = __________ kilometres

3. 1,000 millilitres = ____________ litres

4. 20 m = ___________ cm

5. 5 L = ___________ mL

6. 4,000 mg = ___________ g

Draw lines and drop the unit into the correct measurement bucket.

pounds	Length 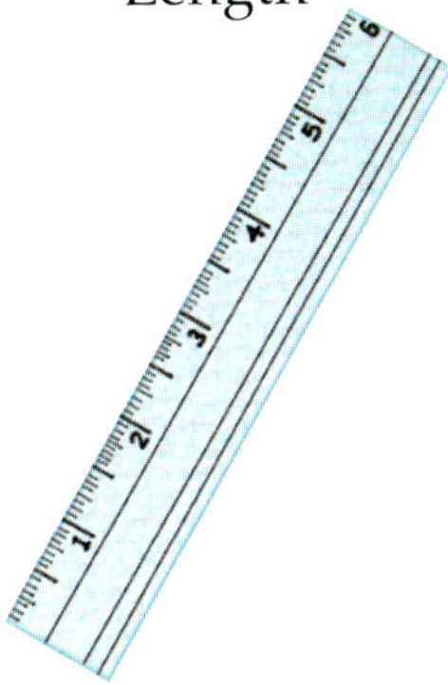	oz.
litre		fl. oz.
metre	Mass/Weight 	inch
yard		gallon
micron	Volume 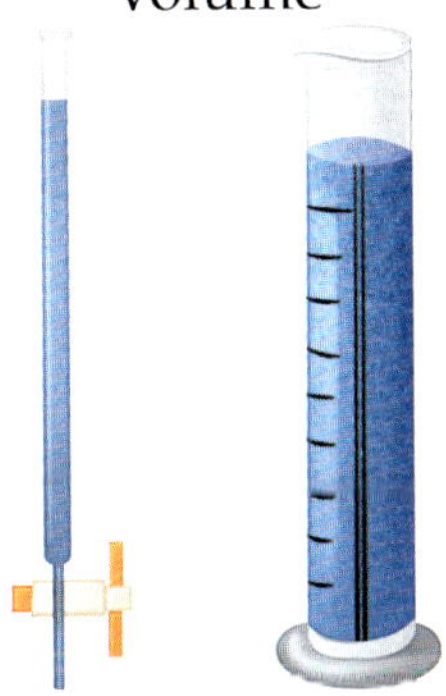	metric ton
kilogram		cu. ft.

GLOSSARY

Ancient	belonging to the very distant past
Balance	an even distribution of weight enabling something to remain upright and steady.
Biggest	larger than other items of the same kind
Concept	an idea
Deep	extending far down from the top or surface
Distance	the length of the space between two points
Divisions	separating something into parts
Far	at a great distance
Formula	a mathematical relationship or rule expressed in symbols
Gravity	the force that attracts a body towards the centre of the Earth
Half	not even or balanced in shape
Measurement	a unit or system of measuring
Precise	exact, accurate, and careful about details
Reset	to set again or differently
Spring	an elastic device, typically a helical metal coil, that can be pressed or pulled but returns to its former shape when released
Vital	absolutely necessary; essential

ANSWERS

Page 28.
1. 9 cm 5 mm (9.5 cm)
2. 10 cm
3. 13 cm 5 mm (13.5 cm)
4. 6 cm
5. 1 cm 5 mm (1.5 cm)

Page 29.
1. centimetres
2. millilitres
3. grams
4. millilitres
5. kilograms
6. metres

Page 30.
1. 20,000 grams
2. 60 kilometres
3. 1 litre
4. 2,000 cm
5. 5,000 mL
6. 4 g

Page 31. Length - metre, yard, micron, inch

Mass/Weight - pounds, kilogram, oz, metric ton

Volume-litre, fl. oz, gallon, cu. ft.